contents

food choice

The successful designing and making of food products requires an understanding of the procedures and stages involved in the production of food, as well as the factors that influence consumer choice. The aim of food product development and manufacture is to meet the needs of different groups of people.

What factors?

The shopping basket below contains one person's choice of food on a particular day. In the basket there are some ingredients that could be combined to make a tasty evening meal – the packet of pasta and the tin of tomatoes, for example. The need to obtain the ingredients for a desired recipe is just one factor which influences consumers' choice of food.

▼ Consumers' choice of food is influenced by several factors.

Other factors influencing consumer food choice include age. Everyone's food choice should relate to their physical needs which change as life progresses. For example, children and young people require food which supplies the right amounts of **nutrients** and energy to suit their needs.

As people grow older, their needs alter. As the activity level of a person decreases, so the need for energy-giving foods should also decrease. The appetite decreases, but older people still need to have a healthy balanced diet.

The level of activity in which a person is involved affects their food choice. For example, a manual worker has a higher activity level than a person with a desk job so may choose food higher in energy content.

▲ *The physical and sensory characteristics of food can affect consumer choices.*

The amount of money a person has – their economic status – greatly influences their food choice. If there is a plentiful supply of money, there are few restrictions on the choice of food.

Attitudes to certain aspects of food production may also influence the choices made by consumers. For example, many more people are choosing products that are organic, that is, foods that are produced without the use of fertilizers or chemical pest control.

Product characteristics

An important influence is, of course, the **attributes**, or characteristics, of the product itself. Different attributes of foods appeal to different people. For example, some people like very spicy foods, others do not. The taste, texture and aroma of food are called its **organoleptic** qualities. These organoleptic qualities are important factors which make people choose some foods and not others.

All the factors above apply when there is plenty of food available, but in some countries this is not the case.

Order of importance

The order in which a consumer places the factors influencing choice depends on his or her specific situation. Price and **nutritional** value are often at the top of a list, but the other factors also become priorities in many situations. For example, when choosing vegetables, if price is an influencing factor the time of year becomes an important aspect of choice, since vegetables are cheaper when they are in season.

finding a need

The variety of needs which consumers have provide many opportunities for the development of food products. Since consumer needs relate directly to the factors affecting their food choice, food manufacturers are able to identify the various groups of people whose needs will be met by their particular product. These groups of people are referred to as the **target groups**.

Food spending

Consumers spend an enormous amount of money on food. Recent figures suggest that every year in the UK:

- about £1 billion is invested in the food industry
- about £43 billion is spent on food.

Manufacturers must take consumer demands into account in order to gain a **market share**. If consumers do not like a product, it will not sell. The food industry is very competitive so manufacturers must be continually monitoring their market.

What sells?

Generally consumer needs fall into the following categories:

- enjoyment, for example ice cream
- **nutritional**, for example a low fat crème fraiche for someone who wishes to reduce fat intake
- economic, for example economy packs of flour or tinned tomatoes
- life-style, for example luxury foods, such as smoked salmon or truffle chocolates
- household size, for example a one-portion meal for a single person, a family-size pack for a family
- special occasions, for example a birthday cake.

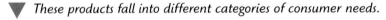

These products fall into different categories of consumer needs.

A saturated market for baked beans resulted in diversification.

Changes within these categories provide **prompts** for a food manufacturer to investigate whether it is worth developing a new idea for a product. Prompts arise from a number of areas:

- a gap in the market, identified when consumers are seen to be asking for a product that is not available or through the analysis of **market research** questions that highlight the need for a product
- drop in or loss of **market share** and consumer loyalty
- special needs, such as gluten-free or nut-free products for people with allergies to gluten or nuts
- new **nutritional guidelines**, published by the government. For example, the recommendation to eat at least five portions of fruit and vegetables a day
- consumer pressure, often to encourage manufacturers to produce cheaper products and/or ones which are environmentally 'friendly'
- more successful products made by a competitor, apparent when retailers report more demand for one product than the other.

Niche markets

A niche market is where a product meets a particular need but may not sell in large numbers. It may meet certain concerns of consumers, such as environmental issues. Organic food was a niche market at first, because only a relatively small number of consumers demanded this type of food. However, organic food is becoming increasingly popular.

Saturated market

In a saturated market a product has been popular for a very long time and sales cannot be improved. Baked beans are a good example. The manufacturer may think it is worth trying to extend sales by **diversification**, offering the product with additional ingredients, for example, sausages.

Food producers are generally growers and producers of **primary products**, such as meat, vegetables and fruit. Food manufacturers convert primary products into **secondary products**, such as butter, sugar, soups and bread. Product development and manufacture have implications for both producers and manufacturers. In order to meet consumer needs, it is essential to keep up not only with changes in consumer spending habits, expectations and choices, and with main competitors, but also to find the most cost-effective ways of producing and maintaining high standards and safety in their processes.

consumer views

The various reactions consumers have to a product over a period of time is called its life-cycle. Some products remain popular with consumers over a long period of time and require minimal updating to keep them high on a consumer's shopping list. Products such as baked beans and cornflakes fall into this category. Other products have a much shorter life-cycle.

Market research

The best way to find out the views of consumers is to ask them! This is called **market research**. It can provide information about:

- current trends in eating and buying habits
- how popular a potential product might be
- the popularity of existing products
- how effective an advertising campaign is or could be.

Information about current consumer needs and purchasing habits provides evidence on which decisions about product development can be based.

Primary sources

Primary sources of information take the form of **surveys** and **questionnaires** and can provide very specific information. Surveys are a useful starting point and involve observing how consumers approach and carry out food choice. Surveys are usually carried out in shopping areas. However, for the method to be effective researchers must:

- decide what information they require before starting the observation
- take notes as they observe

Response form

Name:_____ Product: _____

Attitude: Tick the box which best describes your attitude to this product.

I would eat this at every opportunity I had. ☐

I would eat this very often. ☐

I would eat this frequently. ☐

I like this and would eat this now and then. ☐

I would eat this if available but would not go out of my way. ☐

I don't like it but might eat it occasionally. ☐

I would hardly ever eat this. ☐

I would eat this only if there were no other food choices. ☐

I would eat this if I were forced to. ☐

▲ _These are some examples of questions and how to record consumer responses._

- record only what is relevant to their task
- use their observations to draw a conclusion.

Questionnaires are useful in providing information for analysis if the questions are carefully planned. There are four useful types of questions:

- Open-ended questions find out about the attitudes and opinions of consumers. However, they produce such a wide variety of responses that they can take a long time to interpret and categorize.
- Closed questions provide yes or no answers, or a limited choice of answers
- Structured questions include various detailed part questions, such as those relating to product characteristics.
- Rating questions ask for a person's opinion of the product to be recorded on a scale of numbers or on a sequence of facial expressions.

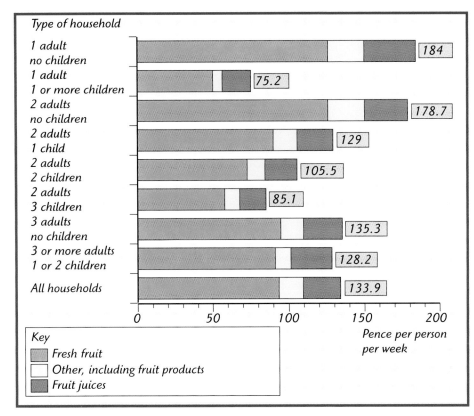

Type of household

1 adult no children	184
1 adult 1 or more children	75.2
2 adults no children	178.7
2 adults 1 child	129
2 adults 2 children	105.5
2 adults 3 children	85.1
3 adults no children	135.3
3 or more adults 1 or 2 children	128.2
All households	133.9

Pence per person per week

Key
- Fresh fruit
- Other, including fruit products
- Fruit juices

◄ Consumer spending. Close inspection of the chart based on government statistics – a secondary source – tells you that:
- the amount spent on fresh fruit by households with children is generally lower
- the amount spent on fruit products per person per week is lower in households of more than one adult.

Two types

There are two types of primary research – **quantitative** and **qualitative**. Quantitative research involves questioning a large, representative sample of people. The more people involved, the more the results of the research are respected as being an accurate indication of people's opinion. Qualitative research involves consulting small groups of people selected from the **target market** about specific products. This provides a very detailed set of responses to specific questions, but the results can be very subjective and difficult to interpret since only a few people have given an opinion.

Some food manufacturers employ specialist marketing intelligence companies to carry out research for them. Mintel is an example of this type of company. Other companies carry out the research 'in-house', which means that it is done within the company.

Trials

Trials are a method used to assess consumer reactions to a particular product. The consumer is given a sample of the product to try out at home. A discussion with the whole family group takes place and in this way a number of different reactions can be collected. Focus groups are sometimes used to measure reactions to specific products. The group is usually a small number of people from the target group together with a trained interviewer, who leads the discussion about the product.

Secondary sources

Market information can also be gathered from secondary sources, such as books, newspapers and government statistics. This is information which has already been gathered and collected and can take a number of forms, including data from other people's research. However, care must be taken to select relevant information only and the validity of the source must be carefully considered.

analysing the response

Market research is of no use unless the responses are carefully recorded and analysed. Information gathered by primary source methods should be interpreted in relation to the development of the specific product so that the manufacturer has precise information about what will sell well. How is this done? Collating the results is the first step and involves:

- making a summary of the responses on a results table or a tally chart
- counting how many similar answers and opinions have been gathered in response to every aspect of the research or questions asked.

Collating the results gives an idea of what the consumer thought of a product or thinks about a projected new product.

Recording the information

This is best done on a computer. By entering the information into the computer as a spreadsheet you are creating a database which can be referred to throughout product development. A spreadsheet layout is shown below.

The headings can specifically relate to the areas of research, for example the age ranges of the sample, or the number of people who had the same response or opinion.

Analysing the results

Analysis involves looking at the results in more detail. Provided the appropriate questions have been asked during the research, it should provide information about:

- the type of product that is going to meet the needs of consumers
- aspects that must form part of the **specification** for the product
- potential sales
- price point (the price consumers are willing to pay).

Overall, the analysis must show whether it is worth continuing with the development of the product or whether amendments need to be made to the original idea.

▼ *A spreadsheet can be used to present people's opinions about a particular product.*

	Question A	Question B	Question C
Person 1	Spicy Indian dish	About once a month	Mild
Person 2			
Person 3			

The following is an industrial example of the development of a new chocolate bar. Analysis of research showed these important factors:

- The potential market – in the UK approximately £50 per person per year is spent on chocolate, although the market is growing all the time.
- Tastes – national tastes in chocolate vary, so manufacturers vary the proportion of ingredients depending on where it is to be sold. Scientists who investigate chocolate say that a chocolate bar should contain 65–70% cocoa solids. The average European chocolate bar has between 25 and 30% cocoa solids, whereas in Britain the consumer prefers chocolate with only 20% cocoa solids.
- Market value and tonnes consumed – in the UK, in 1999, 520,000 tonnes of chocolate were consumed.

Creating new products

Most food manufacturers have marketing departments to think up ideas for new products. They analyse consumer fashions and lifestyles and try to identify opportunities for new products. Sometimes an opportunity is spotted by other members of the production team. For example, a systems engineer might see the potential for new products by using the **by-products** of an existing process. However the opportunity is identified, analysis is a crucial and continual part of the process. Research to assess whether the proposed product is worth further development can take a long time. It is said that for every ten ideas for new products only one will get beyond the research stage.

The cost to industry is high. The figure quoted by food manufacturers for the cost of developing a new product is around £1 million. This is regardless of the type of product, although when it comes to manufacture, a luxury product will cost more to produce than an economy one.

This sketch of a tick-type response sheet for a new chocolate bar is an example of what may be given to consumers who are taking part in a tasting test of a product. The three boxes at the side of each characteristic represent the degree to which the consumer liked that characteristic.

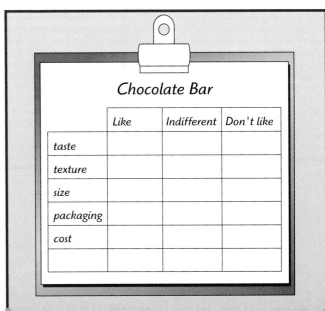

Chocolate Bar

	Like	Indifferent	Don't like
taste			
texture			
size			
packaging			
cost			

evaluating ideas

Evaluation takes place at all stages of the design and development of a food product. It is a critical part of the process and involves many considerations:
- how easy would it be for a competitor to make a similar product?
- what adjustments may have to be made to existing machinery, or will an entirely new production plant have to be installed, perhaps costing millions of pounds?
- can the proposed product be made for a price that the consumer is willing to pay?

The design brief

The answers to the questions are evaluated and a decision is made as to whether it is worth continuing with the product. If the answer is yes, a **design brief** is compiled. It is passed to a design team or marketing department and will include the following information:
- the type of product required
- where and by whom it will be used
- where it will fit in the market.

Sometimes the design brief will contain a specific reference to the retail price of the product. It is essential that the product is made to a price that fits the market. In addition the product must always be of consistent quality. The smallest change in the ratio of ingredients can alter the **organoleptic** qualities and will be detected by the consumer.

The next stage

Design and/or marketing teams investigate all the factors concerned, such as costs and implications for manufacture.

As a result, the majority of ideas are abandoned because they are not likely to be successful and will not repay the investment involved in their development.

The ideas that are thought most likely to succeed are allowed to go ahead to the next stage and a **performance specification** is compiled. This is done initially by the design and/or marketing teams, but eventually other people, such as the packaging design team, become involved. The performance specification gives a list of requirements that must be met, including:
- the type, storage needs and preparation techniques of the ingredients to be used
- possible levels of production, such as one-off, batch or bulk
- the maximum cost of production
- legal aspects of development and sales, such as use of permitted ingredients, labelling requirements
- environmental aspects, such as **biodegradable** materials used for packaging.

An idea that gets to this stage must undergo further evaluation. This includes the production of a **prototype**, when a small number of products are made and tested for acceptability. Acceptability includes whether the product can be made successfully and economically, and whether the eating qualities are what the consumer is looking for.

Research into the degree of consumer acceptability of the prototype is carried out. The results are collated and analysed to provide the information needed to refine the product if necessary.

At the same time, experiments can be carried out on the prototype if it does not entirely meet the **criteria** in the specification. One manufacturer who was trying to develop a layered biscuit product discovered at the prototype stage that it was impossible to prevent the wafer layer becoming soggy and the product was abandoned.

When the prototype is found to be satisfactory, plans for production are made and a trial run is usually carried out. This involves making only a limited number of the product. This allows for any adjustments to be made to the production techniques and the machinery used.

Product evaluation teams

Many large food manufacturers and retailers have a home economics department. This may be headed by a home economics manager, sometimes called a product evaluation officer.

One of the tasks a product evaluation team carries out is testing ideas. It creates a 'domestic-scale' recipe for a product, testing it within the department for consistency, taste and other aspects of the specification. The aim is to see not only if the product is worth further development from the consumer acceptability point of view, but also to establish what the product must look and taste like, so that any unplanned and unwanted changes in the ingredients that could take place during processing are prevented.

Test kitchens

In a test kitchen a small amount of a projected product is tested, a prototype is made and if and when it meets the specification or brief supplied, it goes forward to be evaluated by an organized **fair test**. Test kitchens are staffed by, amongst others, **concept chefs** and home economists.

sensory evaluation

Sensory evaluation is an essential stage in the designing and making of food products. It involves using one or more tests to find out about the different characteristics of a product. The tests consider taste, texture, odour or aroma, and appearance. All products have specific aspects of these characteristics and the consumer's expectations of the product will relate to these.

▲ The appearance of a product is vital in encouraging the consumer to buy.

Taste

The tongue detects four basic tastes – bitter, sour, salt and sweet – each experienced in a different area of the tongue, as shown below. These tastes can be described by references associated with other foods, for example, minty, fruity, fishy. The strength, or intensity, of a taste can also be described and recorded. The appropriateness of the taste for the particular food product can be tested.

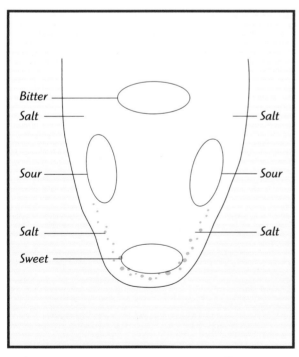

Bitter
Salt
Sour
Salt
Sweet

Salt
Sour
Salt

▲ Food taste can be detected by different areas of the tongue.

Texture

This can be experienced through touch - the tongue and other skin tissue in the mouth can detect the 'feel' of the food. As food is chewed, the texture changes and a different sensation develops. The sensations experienced in the mouth when food is eaten are often referred to as **mouth-feel** characteristics.

Odour

Odours are released from the food because they are volatile, that is capable of 'escaping' from the food into the air. As with tastes, odours can be described by references associated with other foods, for example, spicy, meaty, cheesy, herby. Odours can either enhance the product or put the consumer off.

Appearance

This covers the size, shape, surface texture and colour of a food, for example, large, small, round, square, rough, crisp, brown. The consumer will expect the product to be a certain colour or size. For example, they would expect a loaf of white bread to be a medium shade of brown on the outside. A loaf that was very dark brown would be rejected as burnt.

What is flavour?

The flavour of a food is detected by the taste and odour working together to give a particular 'flavour' sensation when the food is eaten. The flavour of a product is a key requirement in the product testing.

Texture and flavour

The analysis and definition of a new product's flavour and texture are activities carried out during the testing of the product. These activities would also be performed by the testing team with a selected group from the **target market**. The evaluation of a competitor's product can help the team to improve their new product and make it more successful.

More analysis of products

Products are tested and analysed to find out their characteristics. This activity is called **attribute analysis**. Attributes are the characteristics and qualities of a product.

Food words

The vocabulary used to describe the sensory characteristics of food includes:

- For odour – floral, aromatic, acrid, perfumed, scented, pungent, rotten, musty, fragrant.
- For taste – bitter, sweet, cool, rich, salty, sour, sharp, zesty, warm, hot, tangy.
- For odour and taste (working together to produce a flavour) – tart, rancid, spicy, mild, citrus, bland, tainted, weak, savoury, acidic, strong.
- For appearance – heavy, fizzy, wet, crystalline, fragile, dull, round, stringy, flat, thin, thick.
- For texture – rubbery, short, brittle, gritty, open, soft, tacky, sandy, stodgy, clammy, bubbly, waxy, close, tender, chewy, creamy, slimy.
- For appearance and texture (the following words can be used to describe either characteristic) – dry, mushy, hard, smooth, crumbly, fluffy, lumpy, sticky, firm, flaky, crisp, gooey, greasy.

Whether this activity is part of new product development or analysis of an existing product the activity is the same and is called product evaluation or product analysis. It involves taking the product apart and assessing, analysing and recording details about:

- the overall appearance, consistency and texture
- the taste
- the container, wrapping or packaging
- information about the product included on the packaging.

Sensory analysis occurs during the design and production processes of a new product. It can take place at many stages, including the **prototype** stage, after modification, before and during the launch and marketing of the product. It also forms part of the on-going quality check and quality assurance procedures that take place during the production of an established product.

Sensory analysis panels

The people who make up these panels are chosen according to the type of information required. If a straightforward test about potential sales is required, untrained people can be used. Consumers may be picked at random in shops and street **surveys** and asked for their opinion of a product. However, in industry, the information required covers the whole range of product characteristics so certain tests require people to be trained to carry out the analysis effectively.

People with an interest in food who also have excellent sensory skills and can identify and express the sensations they experience when testing food products make ideal members of a tasting panel. These people are trained by food manufacturers as assessors who can then make up tasting panels or, in some cases, can act alone.

Tasting panels can be large. Sometimes as many as 40 to 50 people may be needed to test a particular product. In other situations panels of fewer people are used. It is extremely important to the food industry that tests are carried out in a responsible manner and that **objective** and fair results are achieved. In addition, if the tests don't give a fair representation, the product may not be what the market wants and, therefore, could be unsuccessful.

The tasting takes place in booths, such as this one. Notice that each booth is lit by a different colour. This is so that the colour of the samples does not affect the taster's opinion. The same amount of each sample is put into identical containers, each has a code or symbol attached to it. Only the organizers know which product is identified by a particular code or symbol. The tasters do not.

What is involved?

The aim of sensory analysis is to measure the reaction of consumers to the product. It can take the form of measuring consumer reaction to one product, one product compared with one or more other products, or a particular sensory characteristic of a product.

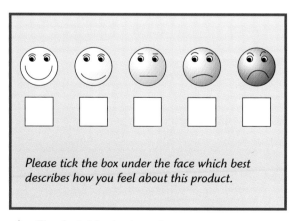

Please tick the box under the face which best describes how you feel about this product.

The facial hedonic scale.

Subjective tests

The tests most often used to measure consumer reaction to one product are the facial hedonic scale and the attitude rating scale (see page 8). These are **subjective** tests in that they indicate the preferences of consumers. In addition the nine phrases below can appear in a hedonic scale when consumers are being asked their opinion of one product. Consumers must choose one phrase which best sums up their opinion of the product. This scale gives a little more information than the 'smiley faces' and is often used in conjunction with them.

- like extremely
- like very much
- like moderately
- like slightly
- neither like nor dislike
- dislike slightly
- dislike moderately
- dislike very much
- dislike extremely.

Objective tests

Objective tests give more detailed information about samples of products. They describe the properties of the product and discriminate between samples. These tests are carried out by a small team of trained tasters and include:

- discrimination tests, which are used to measure consumer reaction to one product compared with one or more other products. They show whether these differences are real or imagined.
- descriptive tests, which are used to find out about consumer reaction to particular characteristics of a product.

making comparisons

Attributes of products are compared during both the designing and making of new products and also in relation to existing products. This involves:

- comparing the effects of one aspect of design or one method of processing with another, to decide which gives the best result. This could involve a particular characteristic required by the specification, such as cost, size and shape, appearance, colour, taste and texture
- comparing the product being designed and/or made with similar products created by a competitor.

It is important to feed the results of comparisons to the **client**. The client is the person or company who has set the **specification** for the product.

What is involved?

An important part of designing and making is checking how well the product meets the specification. Comparing the performance of the product with the **performance specification** is an important check. For example, the flowchart shows a performance specification for a spicy sauce to serve with pasta, rice or couscous. The product must have the following attributes:

- the flavour must be hot and spicy with overtones of garlic and chilli
- the colour must be tomato red
- it must be suitable for reheating in both a conventional oven and a microwave
- the consistency must be such that it coats the pasta, rice or couscous – it must be **viscous** and smooth
- it must have a shelf-life of three months when stored, unopened, in a plastic sachet or a bottle
- it must have clear instructions for use
- it must have attractive packaging, which contains accessible **nutritional** information, including kilocalories or kilojoules per pack and per portion
- it must be low cost.

1 Checking the price – is it low cost? How much are the ingredients? What about the cost of fuel? Check how long it would take to make to get an idea of the labour costs involved.

↓

2 Analysing the reheating and nutritional information on the package; asking questions such as, can it be heated in a microwave? How many kilojoules per pack?

↓

3 Checking the shelf-life references.

↓

4 Heating the product according to instructions. Tasting it, asking questions such as, can any garlic be tasted?

↓

5 Cooking some pasta, rice and couscous, adding the product and observing how well it coats the other ingredient. Things to notice include: does it 'drop away' from the other ingredient without coating it; or does it 'stick' too closely because it is too thick? or is its ability to coat 'just right'?

▲ *This flowchart outlines the tasks involved in comparing one example of this type of product to see how well it meets the specification.*

Comparing products

Product evaluation (disassembly) means taking a product apart, in order to analyse all its attributes. It involves:

- describing the attributes which are immediately noticeable, such as wrapping, packaging appearance, information on the wrapping, costing, the place it is mostly offered for sale
- weighing the whole product and measuring both the size and shape of it
- separating the parts of the product and weighing, tasting, checking the colour, texture and **mouth-feel** of each part
- describing the attributes using appropriate vocabulary
- working out the proportion of each part of the product in relation to the weight of the whole. This is especially useful in a comparison of the meat, fish or fruit content in pies.

Product evaluation helps to find out how a product was manufactured, what ingredients were used and how the properties of the ingredients were made use of. This information can be used in the design and development of similar products and the modification of other products in order that they fit the specification more effectively.

The information that is gained from product evaluation must be recorded carefully and accurately. It is important to use reliable equipment during the process, for example rulers, set squares and other measuring devices to give accurate measurements of the physical dimensions of a product, and electronic scales should be used to give precise weights.

When a product is evaluated, notes should be made for future use. ▶

adapting ideas

Ideas are adapted or modified for different reasons. If the product or **prototype** does not meet all the aspects of the **specification** but is still worth developing, then modifications are made to make it fit the specification. Other reasons for adapting a product are concerned with consumer demands. These change over time. For example, when an existing product does not meet new **nutritional** guidelines or becomes more expensive as a result of an ingredient or ingredients increasing in price, both the specification and relevant aspects of production must be adapted.

Nutritional content

Nutrition is not always the main **criterion** in the specification for a product, but it is one of the main reasons why consumers expect some products to be adapted. People are encouraged to follow good nutritional advice in order that they remain or become healthy. There is a great deal of concern about obesity (being very overweight) in the West, as well as a high incidence of other diet-related conditions.

Healthy eating

Nutritional advice specifically encourages people to eat five portions of fruit and vegetables daily. It also includes eight guidelines for a healthy diet:

1 Enjoy your food.
2 Eat a variety of different foods.
3 Eat the right amount to be a healthy weight.
4 Eat plenty of food that is rich in starch and fibre.
5 Don't eat too much fat.
6 Don't eat sugary foods too often.
7 Look after the vitamins and minerals in your food.
8 If you drink alcohol, keep within sensible limits.

▼ The 'Balance of Good Health' in the UK and other western countries is based on the balance of one group of foods in relation to other groups. The balanced plate shows the proportion of the whole diet which each of five groups of food should occupy. Notice that the two biggest proportions are fruit and vegetables and bread, other cereals and potatoes.

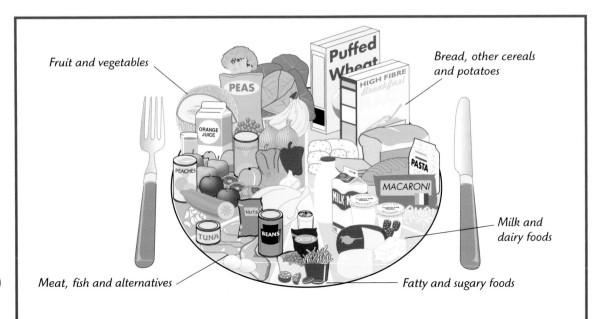

Fruit and vegetables

Bread, other cereals and potatoes

Milk and dairy foods

Meat, fish and alternatives

Fatty and sugary foods

The packaging on these products emphasises healthy eating. Notice they are described as reduced-fat, low-sugar, fat free or as being suitable to use in a weight-reducing diet.

Taste

In recent years consumers' taste has become more sophisticated. For example, the demand for food to be more spicy has prompted manufacturers to adapt existing products by adding ingredients such as chilli to meat mixtures and coriander to soups. It has also led to the development of new products.

Food for vegetarians

The demand for products which do not contain either meat or fish has increased in recent years, leading to a wide range of meat and fish products being adapted. Ingredients such as tofu and soya are used instead of meat or fish in these products.

Appearance

Watching cookery programmes on television is a popular pastime. Although many people do not cook themselves, they expect the products they buy to look as good as those seen in the TV programmes. This means that the specification for a product must meet consumers' expectations of how the product should look.

Fashion

Consumer demand for particular types of product rises and falls. Examples include the fashion for dips which are served with crisps or nachos. This arises from the current popularity of Mexican food, but like all fashions in food other products will eventually become the new thing.

Cost

Sometimes a product becomes more expensive to manufacture, often as a result of an increase in the cost of ingredients. In this case adaptations must be made to produce a product as near to the original as possible at a cost which consumers are willing to pay. Using a smaller amount of an ingredient may be a solution. Another answer could be to use an alternative, cheaper ingredient, but this could alter various characteristics of the product.

It is relatively easy to adapt most formulations, but the consumer must always be considered. The product must continue to meet consumer expectations in taste, appearance, colour and texture.

a design process

When a product is designed, its development is carried out by a team of people. Each person brings their own specific skills to the team. The following is an example of what is involved in the development of a new food product and the people who take part in each stage.

Product concept

The team is made up of:
- a buyer
- marketing staff
- a scientist
- a home economist

During this stage, the concepts for a new product are thought up and researched. The ideas are drawn from a variety of sources including product analysis, analysis of consumer trends and flashes of inspiration. The members of the team research the potential for development of the ideas using various methods, including **market research** and investigation of manufacturing possibilities and costs. This team refines the concepts, making changes to improve the chances of a successful product being developed. They then put the details of the product in a brief which is given to the designer or the **concept chef**.

Test kitchen

The team is made up of:
- a concept chef
- a home economist

Small amounts of products are made up in the test kitchen and tested by the team to see if they meet the brief. These

are **prototypes**. Careful notes are made during the making and testing of all prototypes so that the successful ones can be reproduced. When a prototype meets the brief, a **fair test** is organized by the consumer testing team.

Consumer testing

The team is made up of:
- the public
- a home economist

The home economist organizes tests where members of the public are asked their opinion about the new product. These are informal sensory tests in that the public are chosen at random and are not trained testers. The results of these tests may lead to further modifications.

Pilot plant

The team is made up of:
- a machine operator
- a manager

Comments from the sensory panel and any subsequent modifications are considered. If necessary, further changes are made. When all aspects are considered to be satisfactory, the product is then scaled up, or produced in larger quantities, for trial in the pilot production plant.

Sensory evaluation

The team is made up of:
- a taster/a group of testers
- a scientist

Trained assessors carry out sensory evaluation. Their task is to comment on different sensory **attributes** of the

Notes are made during the product evaluation process that may help in modifying the product. ▶

product. The scientist's task is to evaluate the product to detect any changes which may have taken place during manufacture, such as in texture and flavour.

Scale-up and manufacture

The team is made up of:

- a machine operator
- a manager
- a nutritionist
- quality **control** staff

It is at this stage that a final product **specification** is produced. Further scaling-up takes place in order for large amounts of the product to be manufactured. The product is monitored constantly to make sure the specification is being met consistently. Samples from the production line may be taken for **nutritional** analysis.

Packaging and labelling

The team is made up of:

- a graphic designer
- a machine operator
- a manager

The packaging and labelling will have been designed to suit the product both from the point of view of its image (to attract the **target market**) and also its characteristics. For example, a product which must be kept free from moisture must have packaging that does not allow moisture to reach the product.

Product launch

The team is made up of marketing staff. The public are made aware of a new product in a variety of ways. One way is by advertising in areas where the target market is likely to access the information, such as magazines, newspapers, hoardings and television. The marketing department will sometimes arrange for the product to be launched at a particular time at a particular venue. Often supermarket buyers are invited to this type of launch where they are given refreshments and an opportunity to sample the product in the hope that they will give a large order for it.

Other methods include the distribution of small samples of the product to all dwellings in specific neighbourhoods, chosen as being representative of where the consumers most likely to buy the product live.

In the end, all the manufacturer can hope is that all the careful testing and evaluation has brought about a successful product which will be popular with consumers for a long time.

new ideas

There is a constant need for new ideas for products since consumers are always on the look-out for new foods. How do new ideas arise?

Brainstorming

Brainstorming is one way companies generate new ideas. Employees are often asked to use their experience of working on existing products to suggest ideas for new products. Another example of when brainstorming is helpful is in the case of where there is a need to update an existing product, change its image and make it appeal to a new set of consumers. Brainstorming involves:

- understanding the need or problem
- producing as many ideas as possible
- selecting ideas that are 'do-able'
- asking questions about the ideas, such as where will the product fit, or what can this idea be used for?

Market research

Market research is often conducted and consumers are asked about products they would like to be able to buy. The results from market research into existing products can suggest ideas for new ones.

Ideas arising from an existing product

Sometimes an existing product creates a **by-product**, which can then be manufactured on a large scale. Buttermilk is an example of this. It is a by-product of skimmed milk. Another example arises as a result of an idea to market an already popular product in a different state, or shape or size. The best example of this is frozen chocolate bars.

▼ The results of brainstorming can be recorded in a spidergram like this one for a fruit drink.

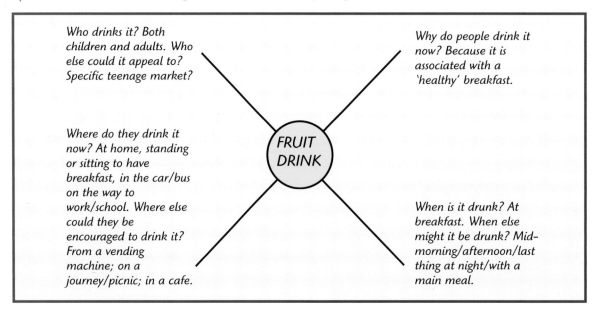

Who drinks it? Both children and adults. Who else could it appeal to? Specific teenage market?

Why do people drink it now? Because it is associated with a 'healthy' breakfast.

Where do they drink it now? At home, standing or sitting to have breakfast, in the car/bus on the way to work/school. Where else could they be encouraged to drink it? From a vending machine; on a journey/picnic; in a cafe.

FRUIT DRINK

When is it drunk? At breakfast. When else might it be drunk? Mid-morning/afternoon/last thing at night/with a main meal.

▲ These products have been developed to fill a gap in the market for gluten-free products.

Inspiration

Sometimes somebody has a flash of inspiration that gives rise to a new idea. This is often generated by the appearance of a new character in a television programme, on radio or in a book, or it may just be a different idea that somebody has. The flash of inspiration often sparks off a new fashion of eating or a new type of product. Recent examples include the 'It's a wrap!' type of sandwich. This is based on a rolled pancake 'container' into which is put a sandwich filling. It is assembled and sold in the sandwich area of a coffee shop or a supermarket. It has an up-to-date, 'cool' image and has recently become a very popular alternative to a traditional sandwich.

Target groups

The people in a particular **target group** are used by market research teams to test the acceptability of a product which appeals specifically to them. Target groups have particular buying habits, from which a manufacturer would like to benefit. New **nutrition** guidelines, food scares, changes in eating patterns are examples. Consider, for instance, the increasing habit of a 'grazing' pattern of eating, when people eat walking about, between meals, often instead of having an established eating pattern. This has generated a need for food which can be eaten in this way. Other target groups include vegetarians, one-person households and children.

Gaps in the market

From time to time a need by consumers is established for a particular produce, which is either not available or for which the choice is too limited. This gap in the market is often discovered by market research. For example, when it was discovered that some people are allergic to the gluten in wheat products, it meant that there was a gap in the market for gluten-free products.

communicating ideas

Ideas have to be communicated to many different types of people. These include the **client** and/or manufacturer, the design team, the people involved in **market research**, consumers and tasting panels. There are many ways in which ideas can be communicated and we look at some below.

Visual communication

Computer graphics and drawing programs are often used in industry to communicate ideas. It is possible to show different shapes, sizes and colours of products using such programs. In this way design teams are able to communicate ideas to the client about the variety of ways in which the product could be developed so that the client has a choice. Concept screening is a way of selecting those ideas that are worth pursuing and discarding those that are not. This can be presented graphically on a computer by showing all the ideas being considered in a box and then showing those that have been selected falling out of the box, in a sort of sieving action.

Image boards show all the aspects of an idea for a product. They often contain wrappings and other information from a competitor's product, as well as designs for and information about the idea for the specific product.

The mission statement shown is for Prêt à Manger, a pre-prepared sandwich company. It shows the use of computer graphics to communicate a message to consumers.

'ADDITIVE'
Any substance added to something to improve it or prevent deterioration.

'PRESERVATIVES'
Something that preserves… especially a chemical added to foods.

PRÊT

creates hand made, natural food, avoiding the obscure chemicals, additives and preservatives common to so much of the 'prepared' and 'fast' food on the market today.

'NATURAL FOOD'
Existing in or produced by nature.

'OBSCURE'
Unclear, vague, unimportant, not necessary, deceiving.

SOME DEFINITIONS
TO HELP CLARIFY OUR STATEMENT

'HAND MADE'
Our sandwiches are freshly made one by one in each shop. Thank goodness we don't have to use square bread, square ham and runny mayonnaise. Our ingredients are irregular in shape - like nature intended them to be.

Lots of ideas
Chilli beans, tofu burgers, curry, couscous, noodles, rice dishes, spring rolls, pulses, pasta, soya products, Quorn™, cheese

Reject Quorn™ and tofu – too expensive.

Reject pulses, spring rolls, soya products, burgers, pasta – too dull and many products already on sale.

A few ideas
Noodles, rice, couscous

Reject rice – reheating problems.

Noodle dishes

Reject couscous – not popular

Why? – modern, appeals to teenagers, cheap and different.

Ideas
Stir fry noodles with vegetables, sweet and sour noodles, noodle and vegetable soup, Thai-style vegetables

Reject all but Thai-style vegetables with noodles – came out best in tasting panel.

Develop Thai-style vegetables with noodles

 This kind of diagram illustrates clearly what was rejected at each stage and why.

Annotated sketches show all aspects of the product with written descriptions. Doing sketches and labelling them in this way is a very effective method of both communicating an idea and also seeing whether the idea will appeal and meet the **specification**.

Written communication

In some instances written forms of communication are the most effective methods to use. For example, design briefs and specifications are written, as are the **questionnaires** which form part of market research techniques. In recording tasters' opinions and ideas it is important to use a standard vocabulary so that the opinions and ideas are consistently recorded. For a list of words used to describe sensory characteristics see page 15.

Accurate communication

Written methods of communication must be put together with great care. The words used to express ideas and give instructions must be easy to understand and the risk of misunderstanding them must be reduced to a minimum. This is especially important when, for example, specifications and instructions about control are being written. Instructions that can be misunderstood can put the safety of food products and/or people at risk. The fewer words used the better in most examples of communication in the food industry. People switch off and lose concentration if something takes a long time to read.

specifications

When all the research and testing have been carried out and the team and **client** are happy with the result, other **specifications** are produced for the manufacturing stage of the process. These give detailed descriptions of the product to be made and the stages involved in manufacture. Each aspect of the manufacture of a product must be carefully and clearly recorded and presented so that there is no chance of misunderstanding any aspect of the process. The aim is to make sure that a product can be manufactured consistently.

Who is involved?

Many people are involved in the production of specifications, such as food technologists, scientists and engineers. All employees are given responsibility for aspects of specifications that are relevant to the process or processes in which they are involved. Information included in specifications covers references to:
- what the product is to be made from – its formulation
- how it is to be made – the processing
- its eating quality – what it is like
- safety aspects.

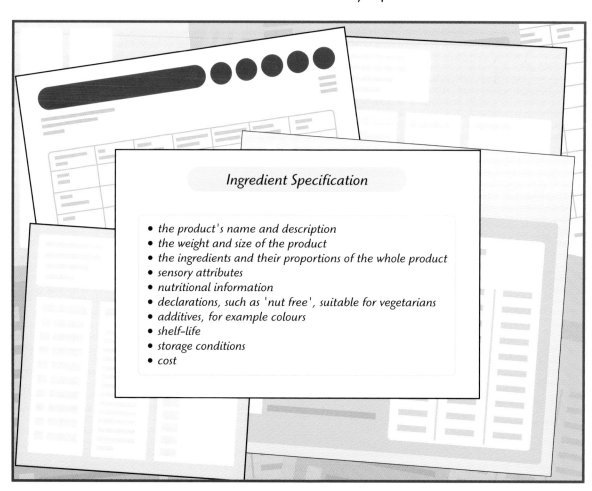

Ingredient Specification

- the product's name and description
- the weight and size of the product
- the ingredients and their proportions of the whole product
- sensory attributes
- nutritional information
- declarations, such as 'nut free', suitable for vegetarians
- additives, for example colours
- shelf-life
- storage conditions
- cost

Specifications are produced to ensure consistency in the manufacture of a product.

Tolerances

These are also included in a specification. They refer to minor variations which occur in the manufacturing process every time a batch of the product is made. Consumers expect the same product bought at different times always to be the same, so the **tolerances** allowed are always very small. Tolerance levels are set for colour, flavour, ingredient quality, quantity or type, total weight and size, presence of micro-organisms (called microbiological counts). For example, the amounts of ingredients for 'chicken bites' may be specified like this:

Ingredients	%	Tolerance level
Chicken	60	(+ or −5%)
Rusk	20	(+ or −2%)
Water	10	(+ or −1%)
Herbs	10	(+ or −1%)

Similarly the specification for the weight and size of the bites could be like this:

Weight	45g	(+ or −2g)
Radius	80mm	(+ or −2mm)
Thickness	25mm	(+ or −2mm)

Quality assurance

Manufacturers frequently check and monitor a product to make sure it meets its specification. The product specification is only one part of the system which ensures that products do not pose a risk to consumers and also that products are of uniform quality. Quality assurance procedures form another part. Specifications for these procedures cover the monitoring that takes place throughout every step of the manufacturing process. They start with the inspection of raw materials and go through to the checking of the final product. Quality assurance systems form part of the specification and are set up to detect unacceptable standards of products at any stage in production.

One example of a quality assurance system is called HACCP (Hazard Analysis Critical Control Point). This involves identifying any possible hazards which might occur at different stages of production and putting controls in place which will minimize the possibilities of those hazards occurring. The Food Safety (General Food Hygiene) Regulations 1995 require all food businesses, where these regulations apply, to build in risk management procedures based on the principles of HACCP. Risk management aims to prevent faults arising, whereas end product testing aims only to detect faults in defective products.

Quality control

The specifications for quality control cover a system of inspecting and testing food products to make sure they are acceptable. The testing is usually carried out on finished products. This type of checking confirms that the product meets the required standard and rejects any product that does not.

test kitchens

In test kitchens small-scale examples of ideas for new products can be made up and tested. The kitchens usually have a wide range of utensils and other equipment, together with a tasting 'suite' and an area where food can be displayed and presentations and discussions can take place.

Concepts are tested out to see if they are suitable for development. A **concept chef** or a home economist, or sometimes both are involved.

Meeting the profile

The test kitchen team work towards meeting the **profile** of a product which has been put together in a design studio. The profile may cover answers to the following four question headings which designers use when gathering information about a potential product:
- purpose – why this product now?
- people – who is it for?
- position in market – standard, economy, luxury or premium?
- personality – traditional, ethnic, **nutrition**- or diet-related, or luxurious?

In the test kitchen of a large supermarket, a team of home economists carry out a number of activities related to product development and quality assurance, such as on-going recipe development. This can be for advertisements, consumer information, or for producing on-pack recipe ideas.

Home economists carry out checks and evaluation of products in a test kitchen. ▶

Working together

Other work carried out in a test kitchen includes co-operation with a colleague from another department, such as a buyer. The aim is often to help the buyer increase the sales of a product or ingredient that is not selling well. This usually involves the buyer supplying the product or ingredient to the people in the test kitchen, who then discuss and develop suitable ideas to help increase sales. This can mean adapting a recipe or making products that show new and appealing ways of using the product. The dish is made up and the buyer is invited to taste and test the variations to see how far they would achieve the objective of increasing sales.

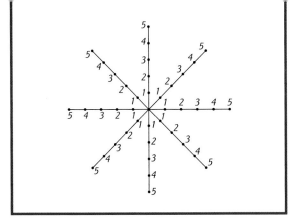

This blank star diagram has the numbers 1 to 5 on each arm. They are to be used to assess the degree to which a product meets a particular attribute.

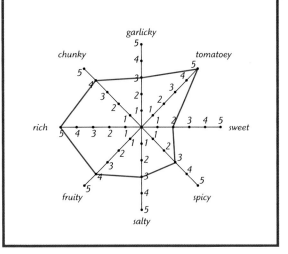

This star diagram shows what a sauce product might look like. Each arm represents one of the characteristics in the specification. The product is slightly sweet, salty, garlicky, spicy and has a very developed tomato flavour. It is also quite rich, with fruity overtones and a chunky consistency.

Quality checks

Sometimes a product is selected off the shelf or from a factory assembly line and tested to make sure it is within the **specification**. The testing can involve **sensory** testing techniques or observation and measuring techniques to check weight, size or shape. It is important to make a random selection to make sure the product has not been specially prepared for testing.

Quality checks are carried out in the test kitchen on a regular basis on all products. For example, in some cases after a specific number of products have been made some are selected for testing. This is a process which is built into a specification and is programmed to occur to a specific timetable. A buyer may wish to check the quality of a certain product, for example, cod in white sauce. Samples from a number of suppliers are drawn randomly from the distribution centre and firstly checked for appearance. The samples are then cooked in the test kitchen so that the buyer can judge the eating quality.

Recording results

There are a number of ways in which the results of tests are recorded. One is called the star diagram method. This is particularly useful in new product development work and when an established product is being measured against the specification. Star diagrams can be used to record judgments and comparisons of all or some of the **attributes** of a product.

Information for consumers

Test kitchens are also involved with checking and producing information for the consumer. The main aim is to reduce as far as possible any hazards that may occur when the consumer uses the product, such as not properly heating a microwave meal. These types of checks are referred to as due diligence (care). This is a reference to the extra care which manufacturers and retailers take to minimize any risk associated with a product. They are a very important aspect of the work carried out in test kitchens.

developing ideas

The flow diagram shown below is a simple method of summarizing the development of ideas. Development samples are produced by different teams of people depending on the company. For example, many large retailers have a team of home economists whose task is to develop recipe ideas for products. Other companies employ a **concept chef** who also develops recipe ideas. A considerable amount of work is involved in this process and knowledge of the characteristics of food and the skills to prepare it are required.

The first stages

The starting point is the product **specification**, which gives details of the type of product desired. The recipes and the samples must meet this specification. How is this done? Various recipes for the product are created. The ingredients are considered and questions are asked about such things as cost or the effect of one ingredient on another, to ensure that the specification is met in every detail. Then the recipes are made up in domestic quantities to provide development samples and the samples are tested. This is primarily **sensory** testing, but other aspects of the specification, such as texture and appearance, will be commented upon. The sensory testing is often carried out in-house, using employees of the company and also a team of experienced tasters.

Decisions about the following are made on the basis of the analysis of the testing:
- whether any modifications are necessary
- if so, what must be done and how
- are the modifications worth doing? Do they involve major changes?

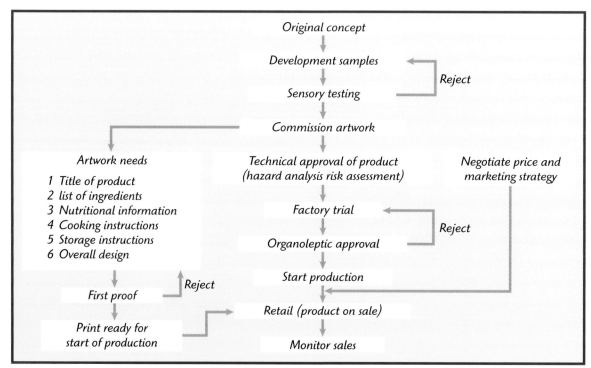

This work flow diagram shows the whole process of developing ideas through to the retail stage.

Recipes are made up to domestic scale so that they can be tested before moving to the next step. ▶

If the development samples are rejected, more samples are made and tested until the 'accept' stage is reached. It is important throughout the development of samples that careful notes are taken which cover:

- types and amounts of ingredients used
- the ratio and proportion of ingredients
- processing methods and details, such as shape and size of product, mixing method and time taken, cooking/cooling temperatures and times
- re-heating (where appropriate), presentation and serving details, such as sauces or dips.

The 'accept' stage

At this stage the recipe or formulation is scaled up in quantity to produce a **prototype**. When and if the prototype is found to be successful, a first production trial run follows. A limited number of products is usually made at this stage, which are tested for things such as acidity levels, foreign bodies, micro-organisms and weight and proportion of main ingredients – a dish based on fish in a sauce must not be all sauce and hardly any fish! The scaling-up must be in exactly the same proportions as the sample. It is often done by computer and checked very carefully to make sure the proportions are accurate.

Possible effects of scaling up

Sometimes unwanted changes occur during the trial run. For example, a sauce may be too thick to flow as it should. Modifications must be made to make it less **viscous** so that it flows though the machinery and ensures successful production. Checks are carried out by the people who work in that section of the process to make sure that changes in flavour did not occur as a result of thinning the sauce.

During the trial run the following are checked by the people working within the manufacturing process:

- that processing techniques are appropriate and effective
- that quality control procedures are clear and effective
- that no part of the process takes longer than it should.

When modifications have to be made, a **factory trial** may have to be carried out. This is part of a process sometimes called product technical approval. During this process the products of a factory trial are tested further and if found satisfactory production can start.

product launch

Launching a new product can be done in a number of ways, such as at a trade show or by a large advertising campaign, or a test launch in a particular region. Whichever way is chosen, a great deal of evidence is used to hit the right market in the right way. This evidence has been collected throughout the production process, and includes the results of testing consumer acceptability of the product gathered during **market research**.

However, if the consumer is not impressed by the quality of the product when it is launched and it does not meet expectations, no amount of clever launching will make a product sell well. Many products fail at the launching stage.

Trade show

Some products, such as entirely new ones with which retailers and consumers may not be familiar, are launched at **trade shows**, where representatives of large retailers can look at and sample the product. Often an order or a deal can result from this, where the product is stocked by the retailer as a trial, to see how it sells. All retailers judge a product by sales figures and do not restock a product which is not popular. Every inch of shelf space has to provide some profit and a product which hangs about on the shelf does not do this.

Advertising campaigns

These are often very impressive and can appear simultaneously on television screens, hoardings, newspapers and magazines. The aim is to get the product name and type into the consumer's head, so that when they go shopping that product becomes the natural choice. The product is usually described in catchy phrases to make it stick in the mind of the consumer. For example the phrase 'Bet you can't eat three', which was used to swell the sales of Shredded Wheat. A television advertisement is usually accompanied by a tune which the consumer associates with the product.

Advertising companies plan their campaigns by firstly deciding what message they want the consumer to receive about the product. They then work on a number of advertisements before deciding which one will bring the best results. It can be a very expensive process. It can cost around £25,000 to research the initial concept, up to £250,000 for filming the advert, and up to £3 million for buying the television time, depending on the time of day the advert is transmitted. The time of day is chosen as the one when the **target market** is likely to be watching, so for example, a chocolate bar for children would be transmitted during children's programmes.

Test region

Sometimes new products are launched in a particular region of the country. The performance is measured and after a period of time a decision is made as to whether the product can be launched nationally or whether it should be dropped. One way of doing this is to deliver small sample sizes of the product to households in a particular region or set of streets. Market research will have identified the type of household or

Try raisin' the temperature.

With hot milk on cold days.

region where the product is likely to be popular. Subsequent sales of the product in the target region are analysed and the results provide evidence about the popularity of the product. The analysis takes place over a period of time to monitor whether the consumer continues to buy the product. Using the evidence provided by the analysis, it is then decided where the product will be most popular and generate good sales figures. The most successful results show that the product will be likely to be popular nationwide. Most manufacturers and retailers employ market research teams to provide this evidence.

Large, multinational companies tend to spread their launching sites over a number of regions. The launch is often accompanied and supported by a nationwide television campaign, where the product is advertised at a time to coincide with consumers receiving a sample product or information about it. However, this is a very expensive and time-consuming type of launch. For example, the test launch activities can continue for as long as a year.

marketing food

For food manufacturers and retailers to succeed in gaining or keeping a large **market share** they must have products to sell which consumers want to buy. Market share can be increased by an effective marketing campaign. A successful campaign will bring the product to the attention of the consumer even though it may not be of better quality than a competing product.

Manufacturers and retailers use **market research** to monitor the buying habits of consumers because they need up-to-date information about consumer trends. A successful campaign will use this information to promote the main features of a product.

New opportunities

Apart from in supermarkets and local shops, food is increasingly sold in a large number of different outlets, such as petrol stations, vending machines and via the Internet. These new outlets arise mainly because changes are continuously taking place in the way people live. The new outlets provide new opportunities and challenges for the marketing of food products. For example:

* the increase in one-person households gives rise to the need for some foods to be packaged in small portions
* the increase in women going out to work provides opportunities for the successful marketing of 'convenience' foods, such as pre-prepared meals
* changing meal-times and eating habits allow opportunities for the marketing of snack foods
* the increase in car-ownership creates market opportunities because consumers can travel to the retailer which best suits their needs.

▼ *Packaging technology has made self-service marketing in supermarkets possible. The shelf-life of this shrink-wrapped cheese has been extended by its being packed in 30% carbon dioxide and 70% nitrogen.*

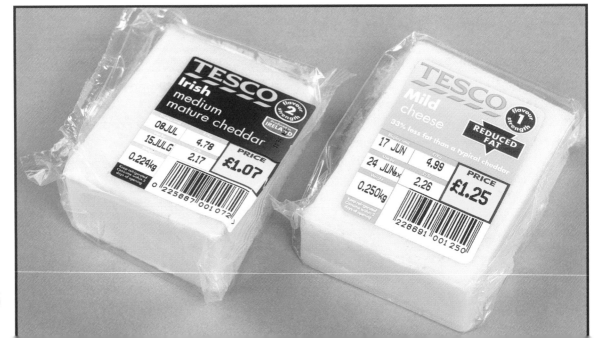

Big supermarkets sometimes hold 'in-store' tasting sessions where consumers are invited to try out a new product.

Technology

Developments in technology have extended the range of foods available and the way in which they are marketed. It is now possible to market some foods out of season as a result of controlling the atmosphere in which food is stored. Fruit is a good example of this. The atmosphere in a store is controlled by lowering the oxygen or increasing the carbon dioxide levels, delaying the rate at which the fruit ripens.

Modified atmosphere packaging helps to extend the shelf-life of products. The products are packed in a mixture of gases, which are formulated to prevent food deterioration. For example, shellfish and white fish can be packaged in a mixture of 30 per cent each of nitrogen and oxygen, with 40 per cent carbon dioxide to lengthen their shelf-life.

Marketing a new product

When a manufacturer or retailer wants to market a new product, they need to analyse their **target group** requirements. The consumer will expect a new product to be up-to-date in terms of presentation, appropriateness for their life-style, in a portion size which fits their needs, and so on. For example the packaging must:

* market the product effectively
* keep the product clean, free from contamination and protect from damage
* extend the product's shelf-life
* provide relevant information about the product, such as ingredients.

Information about appropriate packaging is available from the market research that has been carried out. Certain other aspects, such as the ingredients list and the **nutritional** information, are required by law to be presented in a certain way.

Special offers

In addition to those discussed on pages 34–35, there are some specific launch methods which food retailers use, one of which is called the loss-leader method. This is where new products to the market are sold at a very much lower price than they would be normally. The aim is to make consumers so keen on the product that they will continue to buy it when it is offered later at its usual price.

Other marketing methods include in-store tasting of a product, 'buy one get one free', and vouchers on a product that reduce the price of buying the next one.

sausages – a case study

The market

An independent butcher in a small market town is very keen to extend his choice of sausages. The butcher knows that a lot of people in the locality like game because of the amount he sells and he feels that this indicates that game sausages will also be popular.

The development

The butcher has discussions with employees and they come up with many ideas for presentation, including the suggestion that a coiled game sausage would be worth trialling. The employees think that a different shape would attract consumers and make them aware of the new product. They volunteer to investigate the sales of sausages in other retail outlets in their own and nearby towns. During this research they discover that a traditional Cumbrian sausage in a coiled shape is very popular. They feel the shape would emphasize the 'country' image that they hoped their product would have. They know that any product that contains game appeals to people who either live in the country or would like to.

The ingredients

Most of the sausages already sold are based on pork meat, which gives a moistness to the sausages. Game meat, whether it be pheasant or venison, is rather dry. This means that during the product development stage experiments are carried out to make sure the sausage mixture is moist. This includes adding some minced bacon to the minced game, but this gives a very fatty result. Eventually a little minced pork fat and chopped parsley and thyme are added, which provides the required moisture and also enhances the flavour.

The new game sausage was based on the shape of the already established Cumbrian sausage.

The prototype

A small production run is made and offered for sale on a Friday morning. The sausages are cooked and customers are invited to taste a small piece in the shop. The smell of the cooking encourages consumers to buy and as a result, all the **prototype** run is sold.

The modifications

Although the customers like the texture and flavour, some of them feel that the coil is too big for their needs. Further development takes place in order to solve this problem. The final modification is to make smaller coils of sausage which will provide one or two portions. These prove to be a success.

The product run

The small and large coils are made in a large quantity and are offered for sale every day of the week. The butcher has discovered that the most sales for these products takes place in the middle of the week, the most popular being the small coils, although some larger coils are also sold.

A further development ...

A kind of value added **by-product** develops from the sale of the small sausage coils. Customers ask the butcher to provide bread rolls or buns that can be used to put the cooked coils in, rather like a burger in a bun. Discussions take place between the butcher and the independent baker in the town and now rolls and buns of the appropriate size and shape are also available.

Information on the label must always show values per 100 grammes or per 100 millilitres of food. The value of a single serving or portion may also be given. This example of food labelling is from a pack of sausages.

... and beyond

A buyer of meat products for a large supermarket is interested in buying a large quantity of the butcher's sausages. The sausages would have to be packed for sale in the stores and must be labelled appropriately. The information on the label must include:

- name and address of manufacturer, packer or seller
- place of origin
- lot or batch mark, for example a date mark or the letter 'L'
- bar code – not required by law but a convenient way of identifying aspects of sale when scanned, such as the price
- **nutrition** information - not required by law unless specific claims are made for the product, for example, 'high-fibre' or 'low-fat'.

developing new foods – project

The following project involves developing a new product using a popular food item, in this case, pasta. The aim is to use the steps discussed in various sections of this book to present ideas as if to a **client**.

In order to develop ideas for the new product it is first necessary to carry out research into different types of pasta. The results of the research will make it possible to assess the potential of each different type for the production of a new and appealing product.

Researching the market

1. Research the range of pasta available to consumers. Include different states of pasta, such as dried and fresh-chilled, and the ingredients and equipment needed to make a home-made variety. This will show how many different types and shapes of pasta there are. Make notes about how are they presented and packaged.
2. Look at video footage of the factory production of pasta. This will provide vital information about any special needs which pasta production has. Try to find a CD-ROM which has a virtual tour of a factory where pasta is made.
3. Research who eats pasta products and why. Ask people questions about the products, for example, which are the most popular? Why are they popular?
4. Cook (a) 100 grammes of dried spaghetti and (b) 200 grammes of home-made and (c) 200 grammes of fresh spaghetti.
5. Record cooking instructions and the time it took for (a), (b) and (c) to cook.

6. Construct a star diagram with three arms for each product, labelled colour, texture, taste.
7. Taste each kind of pasta and check the texture of each. Record results on the star diagrams.
8. Compare the different types of pasta and decide which type will give best results for the new product.

The next steps

The aim of the next set of activities is to consider the development of an economical pasta dish which could be introduced into a supermarket chain's cook-chill pasta range. The first step is to find out about existing products. The best way to do this is to:

1. Buy and take apart for product analysis a range of pasta dishes, such as pasta salad, tuna and corn pasta, and lasagne. Look at and record the ingredients, cost, storage/reheating/cooking instructions, **nutritional** information.
2. Research secondary sources of information, such as the Internet, magazines, relevant software and recipe books to help you with ideas for your product.
3. Devise a **questionnaire** to help survey people's likes and dislikes. Ask simple questions, such as 'Do you like pasta products?'. Then if the answer is 'yes', the next questions should be 'What type of pasta is your favourite?' and 'What type of sauce do you prefer?'.

The results of these first steps will help you to think of a suitable idea for an economical product for the cook-chill pasta range. You will need to:

▲ *Pre-prepared pasta dishes.*

1. Make an evaluation of the questionnaire results.
2. Draw up of a list of ingredients which meet the cost requirements for the pasta base and sauce to go with it.

The brief

This will include:

- details of the product to be developed and its packaging, for example, penne with chilli chicken sauce presented with an attractive photograph on the package.
- a list of ingredients, expressed as percentages of the whole
- the costing of the ingredients, and other costs, such as manufacturing and packaging
- nutritional value per pack and per portion
- quality assurance and food safety checks.

Production

A flow diagram, with safety and quality assurance checks included at each stage of production of a **prototype** is necessary to make sure that the manufacturing process is as effective as possible. If the product is made, photographs of various aspects of the product could be taken, such as a sectional view of a portion of it.

Evaluation of the idea

This takes place with the client. All the information about the product can be presented using an image board, accompanied by the finished product, if made. Evaluation takes the form of:

- discussion about the product
- plans for any modifications which may be necessary
- discussion about the implications for large-scale manufacture
- consideration about the type of packaging which might be appropriate (computer programs which enable the modelling of all the aspects of the product are useful tools for this).

food in practice

Shortbread is a very popular sweet biscuit product, marketed in many forms, including finger and fan shapes. The ingredients used for most types of shortbread are similar, but there are differences in the proportions and types of ingredients used. The proportions vary according to the degree of richness, shortness and crispness required by the **specification** for the different types of shortbread.

Research shortbread

Using the results of the experiments, compile a design specification for each product. The specifications would be used by the product development team in a test kitchen as the basis for developing ideas for shortbread products.

1. Investigate the range of shortbreads available. As well as researching in shops, if possible use the Internet, ICT, and **nutrition** food tables, such as those in the *Manual of Nutrition*, or a nutritional analysis computer program, such as PC Cuisine or MacCuisine.
2. Buy three examples of different types. Break and taste them. Evaluate them for texture, flavour, cost, nutritional value, ingredients and packaging. Make notes about the evaluation. Rank the products in the order of the one you liked best down to the one you liked least. Explain why you ranked them as you did.
3. Look at recipes for making similar shortbread at home. Make notes about the amount and proportion of ingredients used.
4. Consider the shapes of the biscuits and, using ICT, develop templates for two different shapes for use in manufacture.

▲ *Shortbread fingers.*

Designing for manufacture

Most consumers expect the **mouth-feel** of shortbread to be soft and crumbly. It is the functional characteristics of fat that provide this, that is, how fat behaves and changes when mixed with the other ingredients and cooked. The type of fat and other ingredients and the proportion in which they are used are crucial aspects in achieving the desired mouth-feel. To find out more about how to achieve this you can experiment with different types and proportions of the basic ingredients.

In every case use the following method. This is important because too much mixing and handling of any shortbread dough produces a tough result and a product which does not melt in the mouth as it should.

1. Soften the fat to a creamy consistency without melting.
2. Mix in the sugar.

3. Mix in the sifted flour, firstly with a wooden spoon and then gently bring the mixture together with your hands until a paste is made. Do not over-work the mixture, as this will give a tough result.
4. Shape as desired. Arrange on a greased oven tray.
5. Cook at 150°C or gas mark 2 for the time which is appropriate for the shape. For example, for fingers or fans, about 30 minutes; for large rounds about one and a quarter hours. The shortbread should be a pale golden colour, and not over-cooked, as this alters the flavour the consumer expects shortbread to have.

Recording your findings

Before you start, compile star diagrams for recording the results and evaluation of each product. The stars should have three arms, labelled 'taste', 'texture' and 'appearance'.

Carrying out experiments

To find out if the type of ingredient used makes a difference to the finished product. In each experiment:

1. Make up the recipe to produce the shortbread dough.
2. Shape the dough as described (using one of the templates made if appropriate).
3. Cook, taste, test and record findings.
4. Evaluate the product for taste, texture and appearance.

Experiment 1

Recipe – 175 grammes plain flour, 110 grammes butter (at room temperature), 50 grammes caster sugar, extra tablespoon of caster sugar for sprinkling onto the cooked shortbread.

Special instructions:
1. Roll the dough out to about 3 millimetres thick.
2. Cut the biscuits out using a 7.5-centimetre cutter.

Experiment 2

Recipe – 175 grammes plain flour, 175 grammes butter, 75 grammes caster sugar, 75 grammes fine semolina.

Special instructions:
1. Add semolina after the flour.
2. Roll the dough out to about 3 millimetres thick.
3. Use a fan-shaped template to cut out the biscuits.
4. Prick the shapes all over with a fork to prevent the dough rising during cooking.

Experiment 3

Recipe – as experiment 1, but using margarine instead of butter.

Special instructions: as experiment 1.

Experiment 4

Recipe – 75 grammes plain flour, 75 grammes wholewheat flour, 50 grammes ground rice, 50 grammes caster sugar, 175 grammes butter.

Special instructions:
1. Mix plain and wholewheat flours together.
2. Add ground rice after the flours.
3. Roll out and prick dough as experiment 2.

resources

Books

Collins Real World Food Technology J Inglis & S Plews with E Chapman	Collins 1997
Collins Study & Revision Guide: Food Technology GCSE J Hotson & J Robinson	Collins 1999
Design & Make it! Food technology for KS3 Hazel King & Tristam Shepard	Stanley Thornes (Publishers) Ltd 1999
Examining Food Technology Anne Barnett	Heinemann 1996
Food Technology Janet Inglis, Sue Plews, Eileen Chapman	Collins Educational 1997
Food technology to GCSE Anita Tull	Oxford University Press 1998
GCSE Food Technology for OCR Jenny Ridgwell	Heinemann 1999
Manual of Nutrition	Fisheries and Food Ministry of Agriculture 1995
Nuffield D&T: Food Technology	Longman 1996
The Science and Technology of Foods R K Proudlove	Forbes Publications
Skills in Food Technology Jenny Ridgwell	Heinemann 1997
Understanding Ingredients Anne Barnett	Heinemann 1998

Contacts

British Nutrition Foundation
High Holborn House
52-54 High Holborn
London
WC1V 6RQ
020 7404 6504
www.nutrition.org.uk

The Food & Drink Industry National
Training Organisation
6 Catherine Street
London
WC2 5JJ
020 7836 2460
www.foodanddrinknto.org.uk
More information on training and careers
in food and drink manufacturing.

The Institute of Food Science &
Technology
5 Cambridge Court
210 Shepherd's Bush Rd
London
W6 7NJ
020 7603 6316
www.ifst.org
Gives information on food-related
training and careers.

Sustain (previously The National Food
Alliance)
5-11 Worship Street
London
EC2A 2BH
020 7628 7774
Publications focus on food and its
production, looking at how food is grown,
manufactured, transported and stored.

I.C.T.

www.foodforum.org.uk
Useful for general information about
food, diet and health.

www.foodtech.org.uk
A site for students as well as teachers that
gives a good overview of food technology.

glossary

attribute a quality or feature characteristic of a specific product or material

biodegradable capable of being decomposed by bacteria or other living organisms

by-product a secondary product made in the manufacture of something else

concept chef a chef employed by an organization to experiment with and discover new ideas for products

control a device by which a machine is regulated

criterion (plural criteria) the requirement or characteristic of a task or a product which must be achieved

design brief a description of the look and function of a product which must be met in the designing of a product

diversification to enlarge or vary a range of products or scope of an operation

factory trial production of a small run of a product using a factory system before full scale production takes place

fair test a test which examines all variables to make sure the results are accurate

focus group a group of people assembled to assess a new product

intensity a measurable amount of a quantity, for example of flavouring in a product

market share the portion of the market controlled by a particular company or product

marketing intelligence information about the popularity of products and buying habits and needs of consumers usually gathered by companies who study and research the market

mouth-feel the sensations experienced in the mouth when food is eaten. The texture of a food material in the mouth.

niche market a specialised, profitable section of the market

nutritional relating to the amount of nutrients within the food

organoleptic acting on or involving the use of the sense organs in the assessment of food

performance specification the precise details of how a product or process must be met for successful results

primary product the raw materials produced from primary processing methods, for example flour from wheat

profile information about the purpose, target market, position in the market and personality of a product

prompt information which causes or brings about an idea for a new product or a modification of an established product

prototype a preliminary product from which further development takes place.

qualitative concerned with or measurement by quality

quantitative concerned with, or measurement by quantity

questionnaire a set of printed questions, usually with a choice of answers, devised for a survey or statistical study

saturated market a market for a particular product or products where the supply is greater than the demand

secondary product a product which is made after the primary processing of a commodity, for example, flour into bread (a secondary product)

sensory relating to the senses, for example, taste and smell

specification a detailed description of the design, materials and systems used to make specific products.

subjective based on or influenced by personal feelings, tastes or opinions

target group the type of people for whom a specific product is designed and manufactured

target market that section of consumers for whom a product is designed

tolerance an allowable amount of variation of a specified quantity in the dimensions and/or the operation of a machine or part of a machine

trade show a show where manufacturers and retailers display their products

trial a test carried out to assess the suitability of performance of a product, commodity, system or manufacturing process

value-added a product which has added features for which the consumer is willing to pay extra

variety of needs the different needs which various groups of people use as criteria for choosing food products, for example portion size, price, particular food choices, such as vegetarian choices

viscous a thick, sticky consistency between solid and liquid

index